MW00895443

# ARMS
## NEW AND SELECTED POEMS

ESSENTIAL POETS SERIES 96

Guernica Editions acknowledge the financial support of the Government of
Canada through the Book Publishing Industry Development Program (BPIDP).

# Laura Boss

# Arms
## New and Selected Poems

## Guernica
Toronto·Buffalo·Lancaster (U.K.)
1999

Antonio D'Alfonso, editor
Guernica Editions Inc.
P.O. Box 117, Station P, Toronto (ON), Canada M5S 2S6
2250 Military Road, Tonawanda, N.Y. 14150-6000 U.S.A.
Gazelle, Falcon House, Queen Square, Lancaster LA1 1RN U.K.

Printed in Canada.

Legal Deposit — Third Quarter
National Library of Canada
Library of Congress Catalog Card Number: 99-64477.
Canadian Cataloguing in Publication Data
Boss, Laura
Arms : new and selected poems
(Essential poets ; 96)
ISBN 1-55071-095-8
I. Title. II. Series.
Ps3552.O763A86 1999 811'.54 C99-900869-2

# Table of Contents

# I Am My Father's Daughter

Tonight, remembering
the shadow of my
father's voice
saying he'd make it
up to me
as he vomited black
into a metal bowl
I held for him,
a fading giant.
He knew, yes, he knew
what lay hidden from him
on afternoons
each shorter,
each darker,
each closer to the end.
"Please, God, no, no,"
prayed the atheist's daughter.
My father, married at eighteen —
a shotgun wedding,
divorced twice from his first wife,
a true son of his parents
also divorced, remarried, divorced,
and his father married again.
My father, a man the ladies
smiled across the room to,
leaned close to,
and he, the gentleman,
smiling back into their eyes.
"Don't die, daddy.
Don't know you're going to die."
My mother, teaching,

I leave school at noon.
Something's wrong —
my mother gives
me her role —
hides in the classroom by day
to face the light at night —
sixteen, and the secret wrapped
up in me —
My mother trusts me not to tell —
my father too —
"I'll make it up to you,"
he keeps repeating —
smiling the smile
that made the ladies
move across the room to him.

One morphine day,
two days before the end,
he stopped being lucid —
his words clearly etched my failure
in the air; over and over for two days,
"I'm sitting on my coffin."
Too many women cried at my father's funeral.
"You have your father's smile."
I am my father's daughter.

# The Candy Lady

Aunt Lily stood
behind her candy counter
passing out Mary Janes, Hersheys, and advice.

Everyone listened to Aunt Lily,
seer of the pinball crowd,
Ann Landers to the neighborhood.

A sapphire ring guarded her finger,
a gift from the man who promised to marry her
but never did.
Six cats slept in her bed
in a room behind the store.
Once she had her advice published.
Publishers put her words to music,
promising her success,
charging her two hundred dollars.

Aunt Lily could never eat candy.
Diabetic, she checked her urine every day.
She used to have me watch
the chemical kaleidoscope: blue, green, yellow, orange.
She was Merlin of the urine test.

After the cat scratched her,
they amputated one leg,
and then the other.
It took twelve months for her to die;
she never sold another penny candy.
Aunt Lily left me a song, her advice, and her ring.
The candy was eaten up,

and the cats disappeared.
Last year I took her ring to a jeweler;
the stone was loose.
And he told me her stone was glass.

# My Ringless Fingers on the Steering Wheel Tell the Story

Never before, without a ring,
The first, gold, with a heart etched in the center.
I still have it.
Still have the memory of its being pressed into my
four-year-old finger by Aunt Lily who worried I'd get
lost as we stood on a crowded bus filled with Christmas
shoppers going down Smith Street in Perth Amboy —
and I, thrilled to be out in the dark among the crowd,
resenting, accepting the protective pressure on my ring finger.

And the amethyst birthday ring from my parents
(though amethyst is not my birthstone)
rewarding me for being their good girl,
reminding me to be their good girl.

All the instant identity rings
the eighth grade going steady rings to show which boy I
belonged to that month; the Girl Scout ring; an Iota Phi
high school ring that proclaimed I was Jewish, pseudo
snob, and couldn't get into Rainbow Girls; and my
Woodbridge High School ring that like my high school
never felt comfortable, though I almost made
cheerleader but left finals to take a train to
Lawrenceville and keep my date with a preppie whose
roommate discussed Schopenhauer (whom I'd never
heard of), his apartment on Sutton Place South
his dates with Susan Strasberg, his producer father,
and with whom I fell madly in love though he didn't
know and came to my Sweet Sixteen and later, instead

of going to Harvard where my date went, joined the
Marines, disappeared — that afternoon was worth
giving up two years of cheerleading for
although none of my friends agreed.

Finally, his succession of rings —
the N.Y.U. one that kept falling off my finger even when
I bandaged up the back, replaced by a huge diamond
marquis, supposedly flawless, chosen by his mother,
a ring that the other Douglass freshmen recognized as a
definite world with a definite picture
of the wife and mother this ring shaped me into.
A year later, a platinum band —
getting tighter and tighter,
my fingers heavier and heavier.

Last month, my fingers once again slim,
the band of twenty years
slid off almost by itself.
My fingers never looked so free.

# Perfect Circles

The best teacher I ever had
   told me I was the best student he'd ever had

The best lover I ever had
   told me I was the best lover he'd ever had

The man I loved most
   didn't love me most when I loved him
   needed me when I didn't need him

I used to use a compass in school
   could never make perfect circles

# At the Nuclear Rally

thinking of my father
who died of cancer of the pancreas
now linked to radiation

thinking of my father
who worked for the Atomic Energy Commission
that ran security checks on him
questioning our neighbors in Woodbridge

thinking of my father
with a pen in his pocket
who could add four columns of figures
in his head but stayed poor
working for the O.P.A.
while colleagues took
expensive presents

thinking of my father
who embarrassed me, singing in the car
with the radio on as I now do
who returned from government trips
with marzipan strawberries, bananas, grapes
who cooked Sunday breakfasts of chocolate
French toast (his special recipe)
and let my mother sleep late

thinking of my father
who smelled of Chesterfields
who never hit, never spanked me
told me he was glad I walked home
with the only black woman

in my high school class
thinking of my father
who would have been at this rally
next to me tonight

# One Man Who Wants to Go to Bed with Me Says, "Poets Should Leap"

Well, I've leapt one too many times
into a swimming pool that wasn't filled and
the bruises though they don't show
cracked me up
and I will never crack up over another man again
though right now I feel there are so many
pieces of me to put back together
but I'll do the reading on Sunday at the Y,
I'll help organize the reading
on Tuesday, and I'll read on
Wednesday night in N.Y.C.
and have even gotten cards
out about it and made calls —
and there's a man nearby who maybe I think loves me,
who calls me four times in two weeks at
night and talks to me,
a private man nursing his own pain
and there's another poet coming on Sunday from far
away to my reading who heard me read once, spoke to
me, wrote to me —
but no, I will not trust a man again —
and concentrate on the acceptance in the mail today
from the *Croton Review* and concentrate on the letter
asking me to read at a college
and I've lost twenty pounds this month
and never, never trust another man again
I keep telling myself
But no, never, never trust another man again,
I keep telling myself

# Last Chance: Atlantic City 3:45 AM

*To G.C.*

At 4 AM  they close the casinos
The pit boss says there will
be three more spins on
the roulette wheel before
the casino closes
This is the third hotel
we've stayed at
in six days
All the hotels
have mirrored ceilings in the casinos,
Velux blankets
The cigarette money is gone
He's just brought me downstairs,
telling me he's found a foolproof
way to win at roulette,
takes the last $10, buys two chips
makes me turn away,
until the wheel stops
He has two chips
on the first and last lines
The middle line is empty
The middle line comes in
We watch the Asian woman
make her last bet
We go to the cheapest place to
eat in the hotel
sit at the counter
I've $10 more for gas
We haven't eaten since lunch

He orders scrambled eggs and sausage
I say I don't want anything

# Surprises

The night before my older son's fourth birthday
I stay up all night
blowing up balloons,
scotchtaping them to the ceiling,
decorating a fireman's birthday table
with the favors bought in the local Grand 5&10 —
with the special coordinated plates and napkins
bought from a trip into N.Y.C. to Dennison's
putting up Pin the Tail on the Donkey,
labeling each child's favor
In the morning my older son walks into
a room with a ceiling full of
red, white and blue balloons,
an oaktag sign reading *Happy Birthday, Barry,*
crepe paper and dazzling balloons,
streamers from the ceiling

Years later, on my birthday, my younger son Jeffrey
takes me out for dinner
Suddenly, Barry walks down the stairs, after flying in
from classes in Washington, D.C., after
a cab ride from LaGuardia to N.Y.C.
for a forty-five-minute dinner before we have to drive to
Penn Station so he can make a four-hour train ride
back to Washington

And this night's sky is filled with invisible balloons and
    streamers

# Passover Night at My Mother's: 1981

With my brother lying on the
bathroom floor clutching his stomach,
the seder begins.
We all sit around,
my son, myself, my Aunt Rose,
my stepfather, my mother, my
brother's Protestant wife (with
the baby on her lap)
reading the service from the
Haggadah — taking turns
My mother forgot to leave
a vacant chair for Elijah
but my brother's chair is vacant —
When he finally joins us
my mother pushes food
    brisket
    passover cake
    nuts
    chicken soup with Matzo balls
I remember thirty-five years ago
my mother forcing my brother to eat just
two peas
My brother, as always, refuses all offers

# Jeffrey, You Stand for Hours

Jeffrey, you stand for hours
out in right field
waiting for a ball that never comes
Your father coaching the team —
his ego on the line with the other manager's
For years you watched your older brother
a mini-hero
And now you, who hate baseball
you in right field
waiting, waiting for a ball that never comes

# I Don't Visit My Father's Grave

I don't visit my father's grave
don't put stones on his tombstone
don't say prayers
don't forget him

# Aunt Henrietta

Aunt Henrietta at eighty-eight walks into
the sunlight in front of her
apartment house on West End Avenue
blinks into the street
Frail as the lace on her collar,
she blinks into the sunlight
does not recognize me from far
Each time now months add
layers of paper flesh
This is the first time
she's ever been five minutes late
She is her 4½ B shoe,
a woman with a closet with
thirty-year-old dresses, with one hundred boxes
labeled
    carbon paper, lace, buttons,
    photos, scrap paper
a woman with a picture of her mother over her bed
a picture of my sons, my ex-husband and me
smiling together on the dresser mirror
"You take too many pictures," she tells Alan my brother
I think of how she covers her face if someone tries
to take a picture of her
how she sleeps with the blanket pulled over her face
the smell of old lace and mothballs
of breakfast always a ½ grapefruit, corn flakes, toast
with two pats of butter

Never married
years ago she slaps the face of a young man who
tries to kiss her before they were engaged,

never saw him again
Another man she's only mentioned twice is a man she
talks of with lilacs in her voice
whose postcards she saved
who died at thirty-two after a tennis game

On Jeffrey: "Jeffrey's sweet," she would say
"Smart too."
If I ever praised my other son Barry, she
immediately praised Jeffrey
whom she taught how to keep records in a ledger
and, despite her degree in accounting, she brings
my teenage son her taxes to do

On Barry:
"Don't come home, Barry," she says
"Do your school work."
Barry sends flowers
Barry flies in

She and I drive to my doctor in New Jersey
"She can go back to her own apartment tomorrow,"
the doctor says
I'm relieved
She'll just stay at my mother's in Montclair tonight
Later, my mother calls me, tells me, "Something's
    wrong"
My aunt who hates hospitals, insists
"I need to be in the hospital"

Jeffrey drives her to Montclair Community Hospital
pulls up with classical music blasting
"Isn't this nice music, Aunt Henrietta?" he asks
It's the first time he's ever had anything

but rock on his car stereo
The admitting nurse asks her her Social Security
and Medicare numbers; I say I'll get the papers
My aunt knows the numbers

Now I remember how my aunt told me she plays
Scrabble against herself each afternoon at four
to keep her mind sharp

This is the woman who tutored me in Latin fifty years
after her own studies in Latin and Greek, a
woman who went to college at night, got
her degree at forty, a woman who after I ask her
why she didn't call me a month ago says, "I didn't want
to bother you."
At Community Hospital she tastes the water
"Terrible," she says

"I'm surprised you remember her," three days ago I had
said to an aide at the Ryan Medical Clinic at 101st Street
where my aunt had insisted we go first
before going to my New Jersey doctor
"Well, I can't forget her," she says
"Your aunt sees the wheel chair and says,
*I don't need a wheel chair; I can walk*
*You use it if you need it.*"

My brother and I sit in her hospital room
at eighty-eight, Aunt Henrietta fragile as a paper flower
sharp as the tip of the feather in her 1940s
velvet hat over her coat in the hospital closet

Now though she can no longer speak,
she refuses to close her eyes for two days

and keeps trying to pull the tube from her nose

I tell her to "hold on for sixteen more hours,
and if you're not better, we won't let
you suffer longer," though the doctor says
she is having a series of strokes
and now she's going into heart failure and I say
she has a living will and does not want
extra measures and he says these tubes are
just to make her more comfortable
and I can't get myself to pull out
the tubes and don't know if I really
believe the doctor anymore

A young nurse calls her honey
works with catheters

"Raise your foot if you feel pain," my brother says
She raises her foot

As if to make conversation,
Alan explains the theory of the *Big Bang*
She stares at him, listens

"What occurred before the *Big Bang*"

"One view is that our universe
represents an instability and at the point that
something became unstable
there was the *Big Bang*
By analogy imagine water being heated
Suddenly it gets so hot a bubble of
gas forms in the liquid and the bubble starts to expand
Same with our universe

It starts from nothing and grows bigger"

Eight of us stand around the grave
My brother gives the eulogy
in a voice so loud
500 people would be able to hear him
The grave diggers surprised, turn to
listen, my mother drops her good glove
into the grave, leans in to get it —
We leave my aunt, the atheist —
who left instructions to be buried next
to her mother, next to my father —
in a Jewish cemetery in Queens
on St. Patrick's Day 1983

# Aunt Rose

As a little girl, I modeled myself after my Aunt Rose, not my mother. My Aunt Rose with her bright green high heeled ankle-strapped shoes, her numerous bottles of perfumes, her dresser drawers filled with black silk lingerie. My mother wore sensible oxfords which she duplicates in child version for me; my mother teaches third graders, struggles with lesson plans and finances after suppers ending with canned fruit salad. My Aunt Rose is the hostess in a Manhattan theater district restaurant which her husband owns. (She met him when she was first working there.) She leads customers into a dining room with velvet chairs where they can have nesselrode pie for dessert. She smells of Tabu and wears a large topaz ring. She has bleached platinum blonde hair and is often mistaken for Ginger Rogers. She gives my photograph to a customer who is looking for a child actress; I lose to Margaret O'Brien. My aunt tells me I'm prettier. My aunt is charming and warm and diplomatic. My mother is critical — tells the truth though it hurts and you might not want to hear it. Years later, after my aunt's husband dies, she has a beau (a handsome lawyer) she travels to Europe with — at a time when such travels were considered avantgarde by single women. Men are always calling her up. She marries again — and after he dies, she still has at least five marriage proposals a year when she is in her sixties. Last week, my mother tells me that to get to sleep my mother counts first, second and third cousins. She tells me my Aunt Rose gets to sleep by counting the men she's known. I always knew I took after my Aunt Rose.

# Acapulco

From the tour bus, the hungry children don't show.
The hill houses pointed out are lavish, used for two weeks a
    year by their owners, privately patrolled by their own
    security force since the police can't be trusted —
But near the harbor, the unemployed Mexicans who don't
    have the luxury of making salaries averaging $3.50 a
    day,who eat iguanas since a two pound chicken is $5,
    where the divers we'll see today leap 150 feet into the
    swirling waves below for so little and really live by the tips
    the tourists give them, as the divers rush from the water by
    rope to stand where we leave saying, "thank you for the
    tips," where they have a lifetime diving career of ten years
    before they face possible blindness from the force of the
    water on their retinas, where the youngest diver today is
    thirteen. Yes, back in the harbor where the tender is to take
    us back to the ship, children like ants descend on us
    waving ceramic cats and birds, their mothers selling
    Mexican wedding dresses — their fathers selling T-shirts
    with Acapulco emblazoned — the children bargaining,
    the mothers bargaining, the fathers bargaining when we
    tourists show no interest in their wares — their prices
    falling faster than stocks in October 1987. I've tipped the
    bus driver realizing he too lives on tips; I've put a single
    into a one-handed beggar's fingers, and when a man says
    I promised to buy from his wife when I returned from the
    tour (and here I am buying from another man) though I
    don't remember using the word promise, I feel obligated
    to buy from him too, and I buy a white and then a black
    Mexican wedding gown for $32, since when I question the
    price of one, he throws in the second for very little. And
    then, a very thin woman approaches me, saying I said

when I returned from the bus tour, I'd come back to her and I feel guilty and buy something from her though it is not especially what I want and she is giving me a free blouse because I've been "so nice"and such "a good customer," and then she tries to sell me more and winds up giving me a free dress so I then buy another skirt with the five singles I have left and get on the tender with the street vendors waving dresses, shirts, ceramic cats, and saying only $15 dollars for the dress, only $7 for the skirt, only $5 for the silver bangle bracelet, only $2, shouts a four year old, for the mobile. They are desperate —

It's obvious by their shouts, lowering prices as we tourists board the little boat to take us back to the ship.

This reminds me of visiting Haiti. All of us passengers going back to our luxury ship, our menus with Beef Wellington and souffles. I've spent all the money I brought to shore. How soon will this memory last when the waiter tonight rolls out the cart with twenty cheeses to select from? "The buys are good here," I hear someone in front of me say. And I remember the doctor's wife an hour ago trying to buy a $25 sequinned dress for $7. "That's my offer; take it or leave it," she says. "I can't sell it for that," the street vendor says looking pained. "I'll give you $8," the ophthalmologist's wife says. "I can't," the vendor says. "I can't sell it for less than $17."

The doctor's wife walks away saying, "Take it or leave it."

"These people are very poor," I say to her. "The dress is worth a lot more at home." She decides to have lunch at a restaurant in the center of town. I don't warn her about not drinking the water.

# My Son Is Worried About Me

My son is worried about me
He worries that I'll grow to have no money
and then no place to rent without money
and then no food without money — (reinforcing his
image of me starving & gaunt)
and then with no food —
a homeless mother —
a few shopping bags — (probably ancient ones from
Annie Sez and Bloomingdales)
her smelling of urine —
her with dirty orange streaked hair —
her a worse embarrassment to him than ever
And so, he declares to her on the phone, he's going to help
her get a *condominium* —
going to erase the possibility of a
homeless, reeking of urine, shopping bagcart mother for
all his friends to see —
for his conscience to wrestle with —
And also after I die, I will
will it to him, he tells me —
and if he dies first — I can barely write that — he
will leave his half to me but meantime he'll pay half
the mortgage — but I should mail him my check early so
his credit won't be ruined by my careless ways

And if he gets married — it's understood
this imagined wife will never be able to get
his half — or would I then if they get divorced
have to live here with her — the two of us —
divorced women — living as divorced women do —
and me thinking if he doesn't like her

and can't live with her
then how will I ever be able
to live with this unknown woman
whom he will divorce and give his half
of this condominium to — Is she worth
my living in this condominium my son
wants me to have —
and I hear him silently saying
remember never to embarrass me after
the mortgage goes through —

Oh, darling son, I promise you,
my son, not ever to embarrass
you, except perhaps in my poems

# My Mother's Toughness

Sometimes I think about my mother's toughness
My mother who has never leaned on any man for anything—
My mother who bought her own house, her first car, her own
    jewelry
My mother who taught physical education in Harlem when she
    couldn't get a job anywhere else during the Depression
And when threatened by a female student ten inches taller
    than she because she wouldn't up the student's grade still
    refused to change the grade
My mother who watched my father early in their marriage
    struggle with finances — working two jobs because his
    penny nut machines at the shore weren't making money
My mother who patiently late at night counted pennies from
    those machines into stacks of 100s
My mother who raged when my father four weeks before I
    was born used my mother's hospital money without
    telling her to try to save his business
My mother who raged all the way to her parents' apartment
    and refused to come back for two weeks or even talk to
    him but gave in when my father came after her — trying
    to explain his desperation that made him empty the
    account — seeing his desperation at losing her

My mother who when she went into a deep depression when
    my father died still took on a second teaching job to save
    money for my brother's and my college education even
    taking college courses at night — though she never smiled
    not once that I remember that following year that I was
    sixteen
My mother who several years after my father's death drove
    every day after school to Roosevelt Hospital to visit his

unmarried sister Lily, never missing a day so my aunt
wouldn't be alone that year it took for her to die

My mother who when I told her I was leaving my husband
(though she never stopped criticizing me for leaving) went
to the bank vault immediately with me because I told her
I had to go and needed her help
My mother who when I cracked up months after I left my
marriage and seeing me like that for six months alone in
my house had me stay with her after I drove there one
night (when a man I knew told me on the telephone to go
to my mother's), had me stay with her for five weeks while
my step-father walked my dog at 7 AM each morning and
my mother made sure I made my college part-time
teaching job and my psychiatrist appointment and
watched me sleep the rest of the time when I was too
depressed to get up except when I ran to the window or
outside to see if the man I loved was coming to pick me up
in his car

My mother who against her better judgment last year cashed
her bonds in to buy my son the flashy red car when I told
her he'd said if only he had that car he'd be able to change
his life (yet she still lets me know each week what a
mistake that car was) though she took my son into her
place the nights and days each week I spend with my new
love because she wanted me to have what she calls a "new
life" (though she does not exactly approve of it) and
everyone else by now but my mother and me (and my
other son who lived too faraway to help) had abandoned
this son
Sometimes I wish I hadn't inherited my mother's toughness

# Firsts, Seconds, and Thirds

## FIRSTS

I was the first born to my parents
I was the first (and only) girl of all the cousins in my family
I was the first of my friends to graduate *summa cum laude*
I was the first of my friends to get married
I was the first of my friends to get divorced
I was the first of my friends to crack up
I was the first of my friends to have children
I was the first of my friends to think money was unimportant
and to leave it with the marriage
I was the first of my friends to believe a certain amount
of money was important (after I had given up most of it)
to have freedom from money
I was the first of my friends and family to believe without
    love,
everything else is empty
The last line is still a first with me

## SECONDS

I was second choice to a man I once loved desperately
I was second in my graduating class at college
I was second favorite of my mother
(She only had two children)
My second child continually told me he was second in
my preference to his older brother
My ex-husband's second wife has a second hand clothing
    store
My mother was my father's second wife
My second lover was never second with me

## THIRDS

Third world countries are among my first interests
Third cousins are usually ones I like a lot but rarely see
Third base and almost all baseball bores me
Poems about thirds are not nearly so strong as poems
    about first and seconds

# The Poet

She is eleven years old
    and too shy to
    read her poems
    out loud like the
    other students in
    this after school
    poetry workshop
And though I have given hundreds of
    poetry workshops at colleges and
    grade schools in this freelance
    life of mine staccatoed by infrequent readings
    here and in Europe
    and there are moments when I would have
    preferred to stay under my patchwork quilt
    than leave my house at 5 AM
    for early morning workshops
    at schools two hours away —
Still, this child nice enough looking —
    but not especially remarkable looking —
    is remarkable looking to me after
    I read her poem just written in this workshop
I read it silently to myself as she requested —
    read it a second and then third time
When this first hour is over, she asks me
    if there will be any older children in
    the workshop next week
I understand that three of the girls are
    more than just several years younger than she
    that they are decades behind her —
    that they may never have her gift of
    perception — her shivering intensity on paper —

her psychological swiftness of insight —
her satiric edge at times biting with honesty —
her luminous endings so I react to her work
the way I did the first time I heard
Sharon Olds read
I show this poem to the college English professor who
    runs this afterschool arts program
She herself has a gifted son who is in this workshop
She reads the poem and almost reluctantly admits how moved
    she is by its ending where the girl's grandmother who was
    once a star as a young girl at the best ballet school in
    Manhattan moves with her parents to Pittsburgh and has
    to leave the school and tells this story to my student's
    younger sister while my student listens combing out her
    tangled hair with the sounds of her parents fighting in the
    background in words this eleven year old "will never
    forget or maybe I will" and ends with the grandmother
    saying with "funny bits and smiles"for the younger sister
    how she never was able to dance after that as the eleven
    year old notices though that "my grandmother's eyes are
    shining as she turns her wheelchair around to face the
    window"
I tell my student she can always call me at home and read me
    her poems or send me copies of them or talk to me if she
    has any questions when the four week workshop is over;
    she smiles At the next two workshops she is still shy but
    seems happy She listens to what I say to the group for a
    few minutes then sits and thinks for a few more minutes
    then starts writing
Again, she is too shy to share her poems with the other
    students and again I read her poems silently and I talk to
    her quietly about her work
At the end of the third session, her mother comes in and I tell
    her how talented her daughter is (something the mother

seems to think — as do most of the mothers of these
students — but seems to want verification from me) and I
add that it's really good for her daughter to take
workshops through the years (not just this one and not just
from me) and important for her daughter to be given
privacy if she's not ready to share her work with family
(especially her mother I want to add but don't)

Our last workshop is on the Friday of the Great Storm of the
Century. This eleven year old is the reason I drive the
thirty miles from my home hoping the wires on my car
won't get wet, hoping the brakes will hold. She lives five
miles from the workshop. All the students live nearby. All
are here for this final workshop — except her. We put the
little anthology together. I worry that I told her mother to
respect her daughter's privacy with her work wondering if
this is the reason this child is not here although I tell
myself it is the Great Storm of the Century and public
school was dismissed at noon

And, after all, no storm is great enough to keep her from her pen
No storm is great enough to keep her from writing her poems
She is a part of that Great Storm of the Next Century in
    Poetry coming someday.

# Waiting for Ed McMahon

Ed McMahon, today is January 24th and I am sitting here waiting for you. I am waiting for you to bring me ten million dollars. You sent me a letter two months ago with my name on the envelope in two inch letters saying I was a winner — or at least that's the way it looked until I read it a second time. But then it seemed that I still had a really good chance of your giving me ten million dollars if I would just get my envelope back to you on time — especially if I affixed the gold sticker with the number 10 million correctly though it was hidden among all the magazine subscription stickers and to even further my chances I took a subscription to a magazine I didn't especially want, and Ed McMahon, I stuck that sticker on so carefully and even checked that I wanted my payment in one lump sum rather than monthly installments, and yes, I checked that I'm willing to be televised when you hand me that check for ten million dollars. And because I was getting my letter back to you so fast, Ed McMahon, I stuck the bonus Jaguar sticker on its special card in my choice of green though I hesitated for a few seconds over the red one. And I left my calendar free for today — no free lance workshops (not that I have them everyday though I wish I did so I wouldn't be waiting so desperately for you today, Ed McMahon). Ed McMahon, I am sitting here waiting for you. I am waiting for you to bring me *my* ten million dollars.

# Proofreading with My Mother

Sometimes my mother helps me with proofreading though she doesn't think I should be publishing my magazine — something that loses money and takes up so much of my time when I could be "paid for teaching" and "have benefits too" if I would just "get certified for teaching," give up my magazine, give up my own poetry, and give up the free lance readings and workshops for something "practical and steady."

I usually get angry for awhile when my mother says these things to me (perhaps because I sometimes think them myself when trying to pay for a car repair or needing money to fix my oven when it hasn't worked for two months).

Yet she still sits proofreading with me — her reading each comma, capital letter, and question mark of a poem now typeset, her spelling out each proper noun and letter of each longer word, her saying "new line," line after line—

My mother and I sitting here working on the magazine the way women generations ago worked together on quilting, bonding together so many different fabrics into one blazing quilt.

# My Car Thinks It's Elvis Presley

My car thinks it's Elvis Presley reincarnated
It's shaking and rattling down Route 80
No one else is on the road
It's dark
And these are the times I hate being a woman

If the car suddenly dies as it's threatening,
do I try to fix it?
Will I even be able to fix it?
(All I really know is how to get the hood open)

As for tires (which I've never changed), I'm
convinced I'm so unmechanical, I think there's
a really good chance the car will fall on
me once I've jacked it up (not that I know how to do that)

So — choices (as a psychologist would say)
Possible hazard light on and wait for
a policeman or well intentioned driver
(who could turn out to be another Charles
Manson type) — after all, I was warned by my mother
and various boyfriends through the years
never to hitchhike and here I'm just presenting
a variation on hitchhiking
I can hear him saying, "I'll drive you to the nearest
garage" or "Let me try starting your car."

I could stand at the side of the road waving
a white hankie (in this case a white tissue)

Yes, I could wait at the side of the road for a

helpful driver who could be a rapist or Charles Manson type
We all know women never stop on the road to talk to
strangers in broken cars (They too grew up on
variations of the don't hitchhike tales)

But after an hour of waiting in the dark in my car
    on the side of a road,
        a road without phones,
            without streetlights,
    with just lights of cars speeding by
and with the flash of my red hazard light
    blinking on and off like a lonely lighthouse beacon
        that's there for all to see
and with my now starting to talk to myself saying things
    like "Things could be worse; it could be raining" —
I'm convinced that only someone decent would stop

And start to smile at each approaching car

# Growing Up in the 1950s

When I was growing up, girls on dates
    didn't go to the bathroom
Or at least I didn't, and
    on double dates I never saw
    any of my friends in high school
    go to a ladies' room in front
    of the guys we were dating either —
Once a guy I was dating when I was fifteen
    said to me, Don't you ever go to the bathroom?
After that I remember going into the ladies' room
    and to a home party bathroom but
    first taking certain precautions,
    putting toilet paper in the bowl
    so there would never be any noise
    from my urinating and then I'd try
    to run the sink water before flushing,
    since the bathroom always seemed to be right
    next to the room where all the guys were gathered —
Once, I remember on a double date
    the guy I was dating went into a friend's bathroom
    right off the kitchen where another guy, another girl,
    and I were sitting —
Suddenly, I could hear — to my horror — the loud
    sound of his urinating
I never dated him again
Which is odd since I would do practically anything
    in the back of a car short of intercourse
    with a boy I thought I loved
    which in those days was the dividing line
    between "nice girls" and "cheap girls" not
    to mention the possibility of the worst thing

that could happen to a teenage girl which
was getting pregnant and announcing to the world
and all your high school friends that you had "done it"
though I remember once, a policeman shining his flashlight
into the backseat of a car where my date and I were
and I was so embarrassed by his seeing us
that I never saw my date again

# The Women with Thin Legs

When I was growing up, I w as told I looked like Elizabeth Taylor. This did not mean so much since all my attractive blonde female friends when I was a teenager were told they looked like Grace Kelly. (I did have one dark haired flat-chested friend who was continually told she looked like Audrey Hepburn.) Actually, I looked a great deal like Natalie Wood, though I did not have (to my constant awareness and dismay) great legs. Despite my legs, which were of the sturdy type rather than the skinny type I longed for, I had met my most recent boyfriend (the summer I was sixteen) at the beach when I was wearing a ruffled-skirted bathing suit — the kind that *Seventeen* said disguised heavy thighs. And once, to my amazement as a sophomore in high school the year before, I had worn short shorts to the shore on a beach date (in lieu of a bathing suit) and my date (a conservative freshman in the U. of P.'s Wharton School whom I had dated casually and inter-mittently for a few months) went crazy with passion — trying to push me back on the back seat of the car, despite the pres-ence of the couple in the front seat. He kept murmuring that he knew I'd have "gorgeous legs" and trying to thrust his tongue in my mouth as one hand kept stroking up and down my thighs and his other hand held me down. I protested and pushed him away, but I was secretly thrilled and amazed that what seemed like heavy thighs to me had caused such passion to rage in him. (Perhaps it also reinforced my growing belief in the power of female thighs to ignite desire in the opposite sex.)

Now, so many years later, my current (and I hope for-ever) lover also loves my legs. He genuinely does. And though I don't understand this, I'm thrilled that he does and don't doubt that he does. But I still take hours to select a bath-ing suit that makes my thighs look thinner (and wear a bathing

suit only once in several years when I can't get out of a beach
invitation) —

   and still, yes still, envy the women with thin legs.

# Sadie and Laura

My mother's step-mother-in-law always called my mother the name of my father's first wife, Essie. (My mother told me this many years later always quite amazed and still quite annoyed.) Then, my grandfather (who died when I was one year old) would yell at his second wife for being so rude to my father's second wife, saying, "Her name isn't Essie; it's Sadie."

"Oh, I forgot," my mother's step-mother-in-law would reply. And this was even odder, since my father's step-mother was also named Sadie — and probably called "Aunt Sadie" by my father's two older unmarried sisters who were called "old maids" behind their backs in that American German-Jewish society of the late 1930s.

"Your grandfather was very handsome — tall and with perfect features," my mother told me. "Your father looked like him but was much shorter. I always liked your grandfather's directness — his way of always saying exactly what was on his mind. You knew where you stood with him," my mother went on. "I never knew what he saw in that woman."

"She sounds like a bitch," I'd say, and my mother would tell me not to use that word — but still looked pleased at my response.

"I remember," my mother would continue, "how your grandfather gave me a check for fifty dollars when you were born. It was still Depression times — though we were on the brink of the United States going to war but still didn't know it. And how your grandfather told me if you had been a boy, he would have given one hundred dollars. After all, you were the first grandchild. And I think with his two daughters in those days called "old maids" and too old to have children — and with your father's first marriage with its five miscarriages, your grandfather had probably given up hope of ever being a grandfather — and of the name Ziegler being carried on. So, now, he had a grand-daughter and though the name wasn't being carried on, still he was pleased enough to make the trip from Manhattan to Irvington, New Jersey and see you each Sunday — bringing along his second wife "Aunt Sadie" who had never had children of her own in her first marriage and was much too old to have them now."

"Your grandfather was meticulously neat," my mother told me. "People would stare at him with his movie star looks — he had perfect features and dark bushy eyebrows and towered over all the men in the family — even your father though your father had his features. I never knew what your grandfather saw in that woman," my mother would add again.

I have no middle name, since my mother had been thinking about giving me the name of her step-grandmother. My mother's own grandmother had died when my mother had been a baby, but she liked her step-grandmother Esther — who had no children of her own but would make my mother's clothes, take her to birthday parties, and read her stories. But naming my middle name after this beloved step-grandmother would have meant that I'd have the same Jewish name of my father's first wife, Essie. My mother decided to forego a middle name for me.

In typical Jewish tradition, my parents named me in memory of a close relative who died. My parents named me Laura after my father's mother who had died many years ago. And so my mother had her revenge. Every time she saw me, my grandfather's new wife Sadie had to hear everyone making a fuss about "Laura" — hearing the name of her husband's first wife over and over and over.

# The Children Are Listening

### JULY 1958: HAVANA

I am standing in front of Batista's palace
trying to take a clear picture.
The guard points his rifle at me.
I put away my camera, quickly start to leave,
afterwards ask my new husband's Cuban cousin
about the political situation
(and about Castro who seems like
some kind of knight to me
and who is marching down from the mountains).
"Don't ask questions on the street," he quietly replies.
"Even the children are used as spies."
Later that night, the Tropicana is crowded.
Cars speed by under a sequined sky.
And Havana will never look this way again.

### II
### DECEMBER 1968: PORT AU PRINCE

The Haitian children have swollen bellies from hunger
and gather around the taxi my children and I are in.
(The driver and my husband have gone off for newspapers.)
When my young sons and I have given the Haitian children
all our oranges and all our change, the others get
on our stopped taxi, rocking the car back and forth.
More hands reach out to us through the taxi window.
I am frightened by them, frightened for them.
Still, after I have given all we have with us,

I roll up the taxi windows and wait for the driver
and my husband to return. My own children ask me
why these children are so hungry, so poor.
They are waiting for my answer; they are listening.

### III
JUNE 1975: LENINGRAD

In a synagogue in Leningrad the young refusenik
tells us not to talk in front of the rabbi.
"He's paid by the state."
Asks if we can meet another refusenik
(who used to be an engineer
but now is a night watchman in a milk factory)
with himself at his apartment to talk privately.
My husband quickly says no.
My children want to know why their father said no.
They are waiting for an answer; they are listening.

### IV
DECEMBER 1985: NEW YORK CITY

Today I hear on the radio how teenage terrorists
at airports this morning in Rome and Vienna
were especially interested in killing the traveling children
to call attention to the children's plight in Palestinian camps.
I hear how an eleven year old "straight A student" was shot
in a Rome airport on her way for a three week holiday
in the states with relatives, how a young student was killed
on his way home for his father's fiftieth birthday
    celebration.
This was the year the children of the world listened
over and over to the hit record *We Are the World*

a record whose funds go to help hungry children in Africa
a record heard by millions
a record stressing solidarity, peace, and love.
It is Christmas 1985 and too many children
are still listening, still waiting for an answer.

# When You Are Grown, Amanda Rose

When you are grown, Amanda Rose,
and fill out NEA forms
(if there is still an NEA in the
year 2024), you will check *minority*,
infant granddaughter, and
check the box *Hispanic* in that column of minorities.
And at your first job interview, your dark skin
will need no check mark when you are
sitting at some employer's mahogany desk
during this job interview —

And, perhaps, by then your father, my son,
will have told you how on his first trip
with your mother, a business trip to Australia,
how your mother was not allowed to enter
a restaurant in Sydney when they stood at the entrance of
the gold damask draped room
because of the color of her skin
and how this also happened at the
next restaurant they tried, and the one
after that. And when my son went up to
the young owner of a Kosher restaurant
and the owner also did not want her to
enter, my son said that he was also Jewish
and how could this man discriminate after
how the Nazis had treated the Jews and the
owner replied, "Please leave." And by then
my future daughter-in-law, your mother, was
crying and my son was both raging at the man
and falling in love with your mother though
who was to know that such discrimination would

spark the romance that would produce you, beautiful
    Amanda Rose.
And how taxis passed them by,
this young couple holding suitcases,
he with his fierce green eyes and
she with her black eyes tearing and
her mascara streaking and her wild
dark hair forming curls around her angelic face —
her almost five-foot frame looking so tiny next to him
(though he is just of average height).
And, finally, at the hotel the desk clerk saying their rooms
were not available because the previous occupants had
decided to stay longer and "To please try another hotel"
and how your mother cried all through that
"dream" trip according to your father
whose own shouting I have always found annoying,
but your father yelled and yelled at that hotel manager
with threats of suits for discrimination until
the manager told the bellman to take
your mother and father's suitcases up to the
reserved rooms and your father first kissed your
mother and decided he was going to marry her.

And I also know that the sweetest, most gentle
voice I ever heard my son use was in the hospital
when you were born three months ago, Amanda Rose,
and he quietly said to you,
"You're going to have a good life."

# Aunt Dorothy

Aunt Dorothy used to bleach my cousin Freddy's hair
    platinum blonde when he was six years old
    (and for years after that)
All the members of my family found this deeply disturbing
    although it was true Freddy was born a blonde
But year by year his hair turned gradually darker
    until by first grade, it was a light brown
He was a handsome kid with his startling pale blue eyes (not
    to mention his pale hair) that seemed almost fluorescent
    not unlike fake blue contact lenses on a brown eyed
    individual though we didn't know about contacts then
It was soon after Aunt Dorothy's husband Marty ran off with
    another woman that Aunt Dorothy started bleaching
    Freddy's hair
I remember how people would turn to stare at Freddy's
    platinum blonde hair — sometimes with the darker roots
    growing in
Freddy was always a great athlete — even as a kid —
So there he would be at bat — hunched over, serious
    expression — platinum blonde hair with dark roots
    showing
I don't know if kids teased him in school because my family
    and I only made the trip only on Sundays to Brooklyn
    where my grandparents had an apartment a few blocks
    away from Aunt Dorothy and Freddy's tiny apartment but
    I know no one ever teased him on the neighborhood
    baseball lot; he was too respected a player

Sometimes his father would appear to take his only son,
    his only child to a Dodger game or swimming —

I never found out what his reaction was to his son's obvious
    bleach job
But it must have been hard on this navy veteran in the late
    1940s when male appearances were so rigidly defined
Perhaps it was my aunt's revenge on her husband who was
    living with some other woman
But I like to think Aunt Dorothy just wanted to hold on to
    something beautiful —
even if it were just hair

# Cousin Freddy

When Cousin Freddy couldn't make a
    professional baseball team,
    he decided to go into psychology
Perhaps it was his native intelligence
Perhaps it was his family background
    as an only child
    a child with a father continually appearing
    and disappearing
a child hearing his mother raging against and longing for her
    husband who obviously was living with another woman
    but would show up once in a while all jokes and
    affectionate and more wise-cracking jokes and Freddy and
    his mother hoping the guy would really stay but he was
    usually gone in a few days
Cousin Freddy used to call my father "my daddy too" and
    though I was several years older than my cousin I realized
    there was more involved than my father playing catch with
    Freddy or my father's natural warmth that included
    Freddy staying with us the summers we were at the Shore

Today Cousin Freddy has a dark beard and dark hair tinged
    with grey (which he refuses to touch up), has Ph.D. after
    his name, teaches at an ivy league school where he
    counsels students and wears a beeper in case of a student's
    emotional emergency

Once when I was having my own emotional emergency, he
    drove five hours to talk to me and drove five hours back
    to school in one day because he thought he could help me
    and though I was really surprised to see him, perhaps I
    shouldn't have been, knowing his kindness. Cousin

Freddy isn't perfect; he can yell at his kids once in a while though his kids are both thoughtful and high achievers (his son Phi Beta Kappa and *summa cum laude* and studying medicine and actually liking his mother and father) and his daughter also really bright who can make her father scowl when she wears clothes that make her look sexy though she probably would look that way in a parochial school uniform

Recently, Cousin Freddy said to me, "I'd never cheat on Marcy even if I were tempted because I'd never give that pain to my wife or family."

# New Jersey Diners

Somehow they were where we
    always gathered —
    late at night, growing up,
    after proms, after
    movies, after weddings,
    even after funerals

We would sit in red plastic booths
    holding menus with 400 items
    and eighteen customers
    in the diner

We would sit in the Claremont
    in Verona or the
    Weequaic in Newark
    (both known for the "best cheesecake
    in New Jersey"), the Reo Diner
    in Woodbridge, the Tick-Tock
    on Rt. 3 (You probably
    had your own favorite with
    its formica counters and
    inexpensive scrambled eggs with hash browns)

The smell of coffee as
    familiar as those diners
    that dotted the
    landscape of the highway

That dot the landscape of memory

# Living in William Carlos Williams' Rutherford in 1959

I am twenty years old, a bride of several months and living in
    a garden apartment a mile from FDU where I've
    transferred from Douglass College (though FDU is not as
    good a college) because the trip from Douglass is an hour
    away from my new husband's job in New York City —
    too long and too far to commute for him
At night after my classes I cook dinner — lamb chops,
    hamburgers, my mother-in-law's meatloaf recipe, steaks
    medium rare in a wedding gift multi-useful toaster-oven
    that also broils and bakes and sits on the yellow formica
    counter of my kitchen and probably almost every other
    new bride's kitchen counter that year as a symbol of
    progress and freedom in the kitchen and in our marriages
Each night we sit at our tiny glass table in the black and white
    linoleum floored kitchen, Heinz ketchup bottle a fixture
    next to his plate, the once frozen french fries usually a
    little too crisp or overdone; I have trouble getting the meat
    and french fries with their different broiling times to come
    out perfectly — I do the dishes afterwards while he
    watches TV — Later we go up to our bedroom, Danish
    Modern furniture still smelling of new wood and Pledge
    furniture wax — A white custom made bedspread with
    matching white silk dust ruffle that matches the white
    custom made curtains that were chosen by his mother and
    me (mostly his mother) I do not want to get pregnant —
    this I know — I want to finish school — this I know
Every other night before the news we make love
I have a marriage diaphragm that my mother took me for just
    before my wedding — the smallest size made the

gynecologist informs me — as I quietly hide my
embarrassment —
But my new husband doesn't like it —
"I don't want to get pregnant," I say
"You can trust me," he says, "I'll take charge of this."
But somehow I am pregnant —
He's happy I am pregnant
He always insists he doesn't know how it happened —
I drop out of school when I no longer fit into the chairs with
the arm desks

# Poker Nights

Most of the women who lived in the garden apartment complex were in their mid-twenties, a few years older than I was. Some were pregnant. Some even had babies and toddlers. They seemed to gather outside of the apartments adjoining ours. Most were pleasant and seemed complaisant about their day to day lives. I wondered if after a few years of marriage I would also be more like them. They spoke about baby food brands and different detergents. They spoke about diaper deliveries when cloth diapers were still the norm. It was the dullest conversation I had ever heard, and I swore to myself that I would never have conversations like that even if I were married a few years, even if I were ever pregnant, even if I ever had children. I kept that promise to myself and instead hid in books and novels that no one seemed to discuss with me. On the surface I seemed to fit in; they were courteous, even friendly when I saw them. But somehow they seemed to sense that I was not part of their group; they probably attributed it to the fact that I was still going to school or maybe younger than they. I didn't fit in and didn't want to fit in. I was burning to get out of that neighborhood chatter. I felt alive only in class. My husband described me as "cute." He played cards once a week with his high school buddies and some of his college friends. When the game was at our apartment, I put out Wise potato chips and dip made with sour cream and Lipton onion soup mix. I would put out M&M's and red licorice. I would put out ashtrays though my husband didn't smoke but no one knew or worried about the dangers of second-hand smoke then. I would go upstairs to stay out of their way while the guys played. All the wives did that, though some of the guys were not yet married. They would make sexual jokes about women sometimes. But that was common then, and women were used to it. I certainly was. I would put on TV, get into bed with my novel. (I was a big Philip Roth and John Updike fan), nibble on some of the candy I had brought upstairs, and fall asleep to the sound of their excited voices calling each other's bluff, the smoke drifting upward.

# Elvis Presley

In the mid 1970s Elvis was playing Las Vegas. I was sitting at a second row table because my husband was an active player at the craps table and at chemin de faire. (He only gambled on vacations but when he played, he played big.) At any rate, there was a stage with two of Elvis' body guards, two burly guys who stood on each side of the massive velvet curtained stage, arms folded across their chests, looking as if they were black belts in karate, looking as if they would love someone, some woman in the audience to just try to run up on stage to Elvis, though Elvis had not even made his appearance. The women in the crowd were in their thirties like me and were obvious with their tawdry sequinned outfits out for a big night. These women for the most part were mature versions of the high school crowd that I didn't fit in with. They were the early teenage fans of Elvis while I went with the student council crowd and college prep crowd. These were the fast girls from my high school and perhaps every other in this country who dated the guys with the Brillo pompadours and sometimes "went all the way." Sometimes even having to leave school in junior or senior year to get married. These were now the women in the audience screaming for Elvis to come on stage. I felt embarrassed by these women of my generation and embarrassed that I felt that way. Finally, the music blared and the music was so dramatic and almost like a musical proclamation of awe that I almost expected God to appear. But it was Elvis, black, black, greased hair, white rhinestoned cowboy suit that looked like he was wearing a girdle underneath to hold his paunch in, tanned skin that almost looked like pancake makeup. He was charismatic in the way great stars are. I understood why those women started screaming louder. He sang with a sweet mixture of sexuality and innocence and pomposity, working up an enormous sweat. He would take a hankie from his neck and wipe off sweat and then stare with audacity and a broad smile at someone in the audience and then toss it out. The women in the audience went wild, screaming out his name, leaping up to reach the sweat soaked neck scarf; some women took off their panties and threw them up to him. I was still embarrassed by these women of my generation, but I could see what they saw in Elvis. In the middle of all this he answered an earlier rumor that had floated around the night-club when a blonde child carried by a very thin attractive blonde woman had sat at a front row table and it had been whispered that the child was Elvis' daughter sitting with his current girl friend. Then Elvis continued his strutting the stage, singing, wiping his sweaty face and neck and throwing out sweat soaked scarves. Finally, the ticket parade of panties stopped. The evening was over. My former husband mocked the women and Elvis. But I was reassessing both. I thought maybe I could have learned a lot from those "fast" girls in high school. They were not so wrong about Elvis and maybe they were right about taking their chances with passion when it struck.

I became an Elvis fan — though I don't think I could have thrown my panties to anyone performing even if it had been God.

# Saint Patrick's Day Birthday Party My Friend Bonnie Gave for Her Love Will

This birthday room is magical
She has ordered one hundred helium balloons
in several shades of green with mylar ribbon streamers
The ceiling of this room restaurant has a blue diaphanous
sky outlining silver metallic stars
The large arched windows showcase the Manhattan
skyline from the World Trade Towers to the
Empire State Building lit up in green —
and the Hudson River reflects these lights
The DJ has Franki Valli on
People are dancing 1970s disco stuff —
I am sitting by myself, a smile scotchtaped on —
I force myself to sing to the music so it will seem that
I'm not lonely by myself —
I pick myself up and go to a table where an especially
homely man is sitting with his slightly better looking
wife — sitting out this dance —
I say *hi* to both of them and say what a wonderful
party for Will this is —
The husband acts like I'm hitting on him and puts his
arm around his wife and refuses to answer me —
I start singing Franki Valli again —
smiling away

# A Love Poem for George Beach Whitman

George, if times were different
(I not so ensconced after so many
futile attempts, now finally in a real love
bonding for these past thirteen years),
you are the man I could have fallen in love with
Not because of your long, lean craggy looks —
the quick pace of your movements as you move
in your tiny kitchen, the alertness of your
responses to all visitors to your bookstore
or to your Sunday tea upstairs — these responses
sometimes fiery, sometimes infinitely kind and
perceptive — sometimes glowing with both
wisdom and, yes, a generosity of spirit tinged
with an optimism that seems even rarer than
your display of rare books lining
your Shakespeare and Company Bookstore

And even the written words above the door
reiterates your spirit:
"Be kind to strangers lest they be angels in disguise."

Today at traditional Sunday tea at four,
Stanley, Maria, and I here at your invitation
You tell us to wait until the others leave
and we will have dinner together — just
the three of us and you, plus your poet-
in-resident who is out buying the bread
You show us your bedroom with its blue silk bedspread
On the walls are books and pictures of poets who

have read at Shakespeare and Company — as we
are to read this coming Monday —
Here are familiar legendary faces with
notes to you: Ginsberg, Saroyan, Ferlinghetti, Brendan
Behan, Langston Hughes, Baraka, Anais Nins

You play the recorder and sing us the
song of the Tumbleweed Hotel above the
bookstore — give each of us a present of
the Tumbleweed Hotel book filled with the
anecdotes of writers who have stayed
here when they had no place else to go —
or no place else they wanted to go —
You tell us the story of
the Frère Lampiere and tell us you
are our Frère Lampiere — ask us to sing along —

Later, I hear how you worked all day
dicing peaches for your homemade icecream,
cutting peppers for the stew, cutting
tomatoes, cutting more peppers —

You tell me eating your dinner at
the cash box downstairs how you
at eighty-six have begun to feel your age —

George, this is a love poem to you
You who know that kindness is what really
sparks this world —
You who light that spirit every night
in this Tumbleweed Hotel,
in this bookstore along the Seine —

You whose walls are lined with 30,000 books —
each a love story of its own,
the sauces sizzling on the stove

# Remarkably You Love me

me of the vacuumless rooms,
me of the paper cluttered rooms,
me of the I'll do the dusting tomorrow
me of the if it's mechanical or electronic
    I blank out
me of the if it's boring conversation,
    I stop listening
me of the unanswered letters and unpaid bills
who sits ankle deep in dust writing poems all night

# Matching Urns

I think how three weeks ago before surgery
I thought (as I cleaned my apartment in case I
didn't make it so my mother wouldn't have a
stroke when she saw my place) how one of the
first things my first husband's
second wife did after their marriage was to
get two places in a mausoleum so they would be
"together forever" (Though in the traditional Jewish
religion I'm still married to him since we never had
a Jewish divorce — just the usual civil one)

And I think how I don't have a place to be buried —
no plot way out in Long Island by my grandparents —
No plot nearer in Queens where my father and his parents
and his sisters are buried with only room left for my mother

What a pain for my kids at the time of grieving to
have to find some plot of dirt to dig me into —
How civilized if I am cremated and save them the
time and effort as well as cemetery trip —
lights on all the cars way out to Long Island
but the air conditioners probably off since the
cars are overheating from the ten mile an hour
funeral procession — No, perhaps a plot closer
to their apartments — but then so costly for them —

Yes, better and cheaper to be burnt up and my
ashes given to them in a tasteful urn in brown clay —
or perhaps pink enamel with little rosebuds with
daisies if they want to spring for it —
to be placed on a mantel

But whose mantel
Will my two sons fight over who will get my ashes —
Will the fight be over who has to keep this depressing urn
on their mantel (neither has a mantel) —
And how will their wives feel to have their mother-in-law
forever parked in their living room seeing the
dust or unvacuumed floors, a constant recrimination to
them — though she was never a housekeeper —

And perhaps my lover of ten years will want the urn —
After all, he is such a collector of cardboard boxes that
his VCR or an electric fan came in —

Will my ashes be fought over —
Will they third me up
So that one might have the ashes of my legs
with their slight varicose veins — or my head —
or breasts —

My younger son who kept his bottle until
he was five probably would get my breasts
No, I see my lover with these —
He always admired them —
Now he can have their ashes —
buy me a pretty black bra from Victoria's Secret
catalogue and throw it in — take out the bra
when he yearns for me —
No, the ashes on the bra would mess up
his place and he hates all dust with a passion —

No, I see him taking my ashes — to the relief
of both my sons — and especially their wives —

I see him putting my ashes in a matching urn

that he selected so carefully for his cat Kate —
I see our twin urns on his mantel —
My fate to be there next to this cat I was so
allergic to in life — seeing some new lover of his in a jealous
fit after he tearfully tells her how much he loved
me after making love to her, this new lover
spitefully moving these two urns on the
bedroom mantel so that he is actually talking
to the cat when he remembers me —
and tenderly pats her urn and calls her *Laura*

# Laura Boss and Her Road Map to Survival

try is Laura Boss's life, in the most literal sense. She does 'or a living." As such, the esoteric, the sublime, the pre-
ıs "zen" into which so much writing is cast has to wait its
while Laura careens from one work shop to the next, fran-
lly juggles teaching assignments with fifty mile drives to
ᵗ featured readings, struggles with car trouble and the ever
htening possibility that she will end up in the middle of
l knows where, New Jersey, with a complete lack of me-
ıical aptitude at that precise hour when the random rapist,
al killer or resident crazy is most likely to roam about the
h in search of Laura Boss. Her manic style, her poetics of
oing breathlessness is a direct reflection of this state of
irs, as well it should be. Style, as the late great Kenneth
ke pointed out, is a "hortatory act," an implication always
. "beneath which not," in short, of the poet's strategy for
ıg.

I don't believe Boss has been given her due. She is no
than one of the foremost practitioners of The New York
ool of Poetry. Employing the eye goes walking techniques
'rank O'Hara, the good heartedness of Kenneth Koch, the
as shtick sensibility of the best pop artists, Laura Boss
ıbines urban whimsy and frenetic pacing with what War-
Woessner of "Abraxas" called the "sexual terror and de-
dency of the suddenly-single, middle aged . . ." I think
essner misses just a little short of the mark. There is not
ugh time in Laura Boss's universe for terror.

The pace of a Boss poem is that of a brilliant cartoon, a
ıderful episode of Road Runner. Being perpetually busy is
ıesthetic defence system in the Bossian universe no less

effective than armor plating. This puts Boss in an American tradition much more rooted than the New York school. It gives her poems' personal the force of a female, Jewish, urban Huck Finn, a seemingly clueless wanderer whose willingness to meet life head on leads to a wisdom much more human than the "vatic" voice and tasteful primitivism of so-called "lyrical" poetry.

Boss's true artistic forbears, her spiritual ancestors are Carole Lombard, and Gracie Allen, Lucille Ball and Imogene Coca, the great woman comics of the twentieth century. This is not to say that Boss's work lacks emotional depth. Emotional depth is a necessity in terms of the comic. If we are to give comedy the scope it has already been given by Joyce and Beckett, Kafka and the Surrealists, we realize it is not simply a matter of getting laughs so much as it is the willingness to create what Burke called "perspective by incongruity." Comedy also exposes those congruities we pretend, for the sake of pride or prejudice, do not exist. In effect, comedy embarrasses us and any good comic knows that human beings will smile in embarrassment and self defence just as quickly as they will out of amusement.

Laura Boss is a master of what I call the saber cut, a comic technique whereby the victim has no idea he is being skewered until he takes a drink of water and leaks from all wounds. Her scathing wit is hidden behind the digressive, flighty, run on style of her voice, a voice, by the way, that annoys some "poetry lovers" because they have tin ears and can hear only the lyrical strains of "serious" poetry (Anna Akhmatova, Louise Gluck, all that jazz). Consider this excerpt from, "The Women With Thin Legs":

When I was growing up, I was told I looked like Elizabeth Taylor. This did not mean so much since all my attractive blonde female friends when I was a teenager were told they looked like Grace Kelly (I did have one dark haired, flat chested friend who was told she looked like Audrey Hepburn).

In a breezy, effortless, chatty instant, Boss exposes both the sexism and the sex pot as assembly line floor model essence of the 1950s. But Boss is no raging prophet. She is a pioneer of the sort of in your face feminism by which a woman keeps her nails long, her make up fresh, and her powder dry while not feeling the least bit obligated to fight sexism by becoming a qualified male. She epitomizes an unashamedly female sense, not the voice of the victim or the separatist, but of an American dame on the order of the great 1930s and 1940s actresses.

Compare the above excerpt from Boss's poem with this bit of dialogue spoken by Carole Lombard in the film *Nothing Sacred.* Lombard plays a young woman from Warsaw, Vermont, who has just discovered that the doctor at the factory where she labors has mis-diagnosed her "radium poisoning." She isn't going to die, after all, news she takes with hilarious ambivalence:

You know . . . I don't know what I'm so happy about Enoch . . .You sort of spoiled my trip. I was going to take that two hundred dollars you get for dying in Warsaw and go to New York and die happy and now I have to stay in Warsaw . . . I don't know which I am — happy or miserable. . . Thanks for all your trouble. I'm terribly grateful, Enoch . . . although it's kind of startling to be brought to life twice and each time, in Warsaw . . .

True the dialogue was written by a man, the wonderful Ben Hecht, but it would not have been possible unless the type of woman Carole Lombard embodied did not already exist: The savvy, no holds barred, delightfully kinetic American woman. Henry James wrote of her. Edith Wharton improved on James. Gay men have envied and imitated her for decades. Straight men have fallen hopelessly in love with her. Unfortunately, the culture buried her alive and left her for dead sometime after World War II.

She was not killed off merely by the right wing cold war reactionaries. I only wish that were so. The left wing, 1950s and 1960s counter culture, the misogynist beat culture, also had a big hand in her demise and we will get no where near the truth until we see how total the marginalization of women both to the right and left was during that period.

Without this genuine and native feminine voice, without this true woman's language, the early sixties feminists were forced to assume the vocabulary and nomenclature of male leftist activism: largely devoid of wit, strong on anger and weak on eloquence, a language Adrienne Rich knew to be inadequate but couldn't herself, completely refute.

Laura Boss, then, is definitely taking back the language for women. She creates a means of self empowerment based on stealth and the virtues of comic energy. But does the snob factor, the cult of seriousness obscure the accomplishment. No doubt. American is both anti-intellectual and, at the same time, intellectually pretentious. I doubt if anyone has done an adequate and fully realized study of the complex verbal wizardry of Gracie Allen, of how Allen used circumlocution, digression, double talk to subvert power structures. And what about Moms Mabley? No good feminist should go forth into the world without the full weaponry of America's great women comics. Include in that armory such utterly diverse figures as Dorothy Parker and Flannery O'Connor, Grace

Paley and Anne Sexton and you begin to see a strategy for survival and autonomy whose roots are deep and whose achievement is vast.

There is a verbal slapstick, a use of language as subterfuge the great practitioners of which have been largely women. Laura Boss belongs to that tradition.

Of course, tin ears being what they are, most people, in the full e.e. cummings sense of "most people," do not allow poetry and shtick to be put in the same room together. Sure, there is Russel Edson and Kenneth Koch, but who is brave enough to call what they do shtick? Grace Paley is often doing shtick in her best stories. Shtick and poetry are both dependent on the sound of words, the pacing and delivery of words, a sense of timing. Change one word in a great joke and you do it irreparable damage. The most difficult and accomplished shtick seems to be coming unbidden from the mouth of the comic, language that, like Joe DiMaggio, makes every catch seem effortless.

But the grace of a Gracie Allen or a Grace Paley is even more complex since it mimics clumsiness, the off hand, the off the cuff. Laura Boss's verbal strategy belongs to this school of shtick. But why then, cries the average lyrical poet, call it poetry?

I said Laura takes from this tradition. Good poets steal the language from whatever tree in which it happens to roost. Liveliness, vigor, what Dante called the "noble" speech of the nursery may be found in bars, on the bus, in whore houses, on really good T.V. sitcoms, just about anywhere except in the bleached, blanched semiotic halls of academia. Spare us the language poets and the Neo-formalists who won't admit their poems are "routines." Poetry does not become stand-up by stealing from it. Hal Sirowitz is a funny man, but he is using the tools of the joke rather than being a comic. He is ritualizing the language of the joke in order to make poems just as a

Haiku master ritualizes the language of what is simply there, the non-judged image in order to imply the eternal principal beneath.

Laura Boss uses the run on, the chatty, the self denigrative the same way other poets use sonnet form or metaphor. It is her technique, her strategy, and it is every bit as complex.

Laura has been mistakenly branded a confessionalist. True confessionalism sees the sub-conscious process of personal experience as a means by which to deepen the complexity of language. Like deep imagism and surrealism as well as Bly's reaction against a poetics of the overly rational, the confessionalist seeks to transcend the linear, the left brained and merely representational and enter the realm of the Ur language, the primal "word," the circle of ritualized being. It is part and parcel with all the strains of Romanticism since Wordsworth, a rallying cry against a world that continues to sell its soul to prose.

The language of such poetry is usually highly ritualized, incantatory, rhapsodic, "primal," a language of dream and nightmare and childhood. It is not so much about personal revelation as it is about using the process of personal revelation as a means for ritualizing speech. In effect, it is the stylization of the personal and, thereby, the exploitation of the personal for the sake of abstracting it into art.

Plath is not having a share session on the Oprah show. Anne Sexton is not doing girl talk except insofar as she fearlessly insists as any great comic intelligence does on mentioning those parts of the body and those acts of the body we are taught to disown.

Laura Boss is far too candid, far too down to earth to be a confessionalist. She does not ritualize the human voice, does not present archetypal images in the manner of Gluck nor does she create rhapsodic litanies in the style of Bridget Pegeen Kelly. Boss is not afraid to sound prosy. She does not have that inferiority complex of the poet in an unpoetic age hell bent on resisting the art of story telling.

Laura tells stories. She dishes, says some outrageous things about herself that are unapologetically in poor taste. Hers is a human voice, a flawed personal, Falstaff instead of Hamlet, but in an age when the Hamlets with their idealism and cult of purity and longing for the primal have managed to bring us to the brink of annihilation, perhaps Falstaff is the greater and kinder alternative: Disreputable, tasteless, embarrassing, without one redeeming virtue save that he gets no one killed including himself, delights us with his mis-adventures and dies in bed.

Discretion is the better part of valor. So is indiscretion, at least in the sense that Laura Boss promotes it in her unwieldy, tumultuous, frantic and wonderfully vivid poems. When we stop being snobs and realize the value of the comic vision as equipment for living, we will begin to appreciate the poetry of Laura Boss as no less than a map to survival. She is on the roadside in her undependable broken down car smiling to beat the band. She is convinced that "only someone decent would stop." Her faith is directly into the teeth of the prevailing facts. Somehow I'm convinced she's right.

Joe Weil
*The Paterson Literary Review 1998*

# Acknowledgments

Acknowledgment is due, with thanks, to the editors and publishers of the following periodicals and anthologies where some of these poems appeared: *The New York Times; Abraxas; Ambit #17 (*England); *Aquarian; Blind Alleys; Croton Review; Footwork: The Paterson Literary Review; The Greenfield Review; Home Planet News; Journal of New Jersey Poets; Lips; Louisville Review; Lunch; Poetry Society of America's Newsletter* (publication of the Gordon Barber Memorial Award poem, "The Poet"); *Soujourner; Talisman; Trapani Nuova (Sicily); The Thomas Wolfe Review; Under a Gull's Wing* (Down the Shore Press, 1996); *Unsettling America* (Viking/Penguin, 1994); *Outsiders* (Milkweed Editions, 1999); and *Identity Lessons* (Penguin/Putnam, 1999).

Some of these poems appeared in my books *Stripping,* (Chantry Press, 1982); *On the Edge of the Hudson* (Cross-Cultural Communications, 1986; second edition, 1989); and *Reports from the Front* (Cross-Cultural Communications, 1995).

I am grateful to the New Jersey State Council on the Arts/Department of State for 1986, 1992, and 1999 Creative Writing Fellowships in Poetry which gave me the time to complete this manuscript.

# About the Author

Laura Boss, a national award-winning poet, is a first prize winner in Poetry Society of America's Gordon Barber Poetry Contest and in 1998 was one of ten finalists in the country in PSA's Alice Fay Di Castagnola contest for a manuscript. Founder and editor of *Lips* poetry magazine, she was the sole representative of the USA in 1987 at the XXVI Annual International Struga Poetry Readings in Yugoslavia. Her awards for her own poetry also include an American Literary Translators Award (funded through the National Endowment for the Arts) for her book *On the Edge of the Hudson* to be translated into a bi-lingual (English-Italian) edition; and Fellowships in Creative Writing (Poetry) from the New Jersey State Council on the Arts/Department of State in 1999, 1992, and 1986. Her books of poetry include *Stripping* (Chantry Press, 1982), the ALTA award-winning *On the Edge of the Hudson* (Cross-Cultural Communications, 1986), and *Reports from the Front* (Cross-Cultural Communications, 1995) which was nominated for an American Book Award. Her poetry most recently appeared in *The New York Times*.